Toothless!

by Jenny Dobbie

illustrated by Craig Smith

Harcourt Achieve

Rigby • Saxon • Steck-Vaughn

www.HarcourtAchieve.com
1.800.531.5015

Characters

Lucy and her dog, Barney

Grandpa

Contents

Chapter 1

Easy Surfer

Lucy's grandfather loved to surf. He could ride the tube all day long! Grandpa was a surfing legend. He had a room filled with trophies. He had won them in surfing competitions all over the world.

"Surf's up! It's eight foot and pumping!" he'd say. Then he'd jog to the water with his surfboard under his arm.

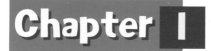

Paddling out to catch the waves sometimes made Grandpa tired. So Lucy locked herself in her inventor's workshop. The next day, she had invented something just for him.

"An automatic paddling surfboard! Cool!" gasped Grandpa. He gave a big, white, toothy grin. "Lucy, you're the best inventor! No more paddling for me!"

Lucy had invented lots of things. She had invented a gadget called *Doggie's Little Helper* for her dog, Barney. It found Barney's buried bones for him. She had invented a machine called *Crazy Cleaner* for her brother, Sam. It followed him around cleaning up his mess.

All of Lucy's inventions had names. "This one," she told Grandpa, "is called *The Easy Surfer.*"

"Terrific name, Lucy," Grandpa said. He was so excited he wanted to take *The Easy Surfer* for a test run right away.

Chapter 2

Teeth Wipeout

When Grandpa and Lucy arrived at the beach, Grandpa raced down to the water. He hopped onto *The Easy Surfer* and set the control to "paddle." Then he headed out to where the waves were breaking.

"Watch me!" Grandpa shouted to Lucy as he rode a wave on *The Easy Surfer*.

Next he set the control to "fast paddle" and headed out to the big swell. He went way, way out from the shore.

"Be careful, Grandpa!" shouted Lucy as he surfed into shore.

Grandpa grinned his big, white, toothy grin and zipped back out to catch another wave. "This is awesome! Check this out," he yelled.

Grandpa set the dial on *The Easy Surfer* to "paddle." Then he put his hands on each side of the board. Slowly he lifted his legs straight up into the air.

Lucy stared, amazed. Grandpa was doing a handstand!

"Grandpa," yelled Lucy, "look out!" A gigantic wave was breaking just behind him.

"No worries," called Grandpa, still standing on his hands. He pushed the dial with his nose. "I'll just set the dial to 'paddle fast.' I'll be out of here in a jiffy!"

Uh, oh! Grandpa had pushed the dial to "reverse." He was heading backwards into the wave!

"Whoa!" yelled Grandpa as he shot up the crest of the wave and flew high into the air. His arms and legs flapped madly.

"Look out below!" he shouted as he fell into the churning surf. The waves tossed him around until finally he was dumped onto the beach.

"Wipeout!" spluttered Grandpa as he dragged
The Easy Surfer up the beach.

"Grandpa, are you OK?" asked Lucy.

"I'm fine," said Grandpa as he wiped the water
from his face. He felt his mouth.
"Oh, no! I've lost my false teeth!"

Everyone on the beach searched for Grandpa's false teeth. A boy found a gigantic pair of orange undies. The lifeguard found an old, rusty shopping cart. But no one could find Grandpa's teeth.

"It's hopeless. They're lost forever. I'll have to get a new set," grumbled Grandpa. "I hate getting new teeth. They're always so uncomfortable."

"Would you like to try a set from our lost-and-found box?" asked the lifeguard.

Grandpa turned green. "Ugh! No thanks!" He sighed, "I'd better go call the dentist."

"I know," said Lucy. "We'll get Sam's *Crazy Cleaner* to search for your teeth. It will find them."

Grandpa beamed. "Great idea, Lucy," he said.

Chapter 3

Cleaning Like Crazy

Grandpa and Lucy wheeled *Crazy Cleaner* down to the beach. Lucy set its dials to "underwater" and "pick up." She pushed it into the water and turned it on. *Crazy Cleaner* chugged through the surf.

"Now we'll find your teeth," said Lucy.

"Is it supposed to spurt out steam like that?" asked Grandpa. Steam was pouring from *Crazy Cleaner's* engine.

"Oh, no! Something's wrong," said Lucy. "Look! It's heading up the beach!" *Crazy Cleaner* was chugging over the sand toward them.

"Watch out!" shouted Grandpa. They ducked as *Crazy Cleaner* threw a hat at them and then an umbrella.

Crazy Cleaner rumbled along the beach. It grabbed towels, surfboards, and whatever else it could find and then hurled them away again.

"Take cover, everyone!" yelled Grandpa as a beach chair came flying through the air. "It's going to explode!"

Crazy Cleaner didn't explode. Suddenly it stopped still and sat hissing quietly. Lucy tiptoed closer to take a look.

"Be careful, Lucy," said Grandpa, following her.

"It's broken," she said, fiddling with the dials.

"Never mind, Lucy. Thanks for trying," said Grandpa. He gave her a gummy smile. "I think I'd better get a new set of teeth."

Lucy patted Grandpa on the back. "Don't worry, Grandpa. I've got another idea. I just need to make a few changes to *Doggie's Little Helper.*"

The next day, Grandpa and Lucy arrived at the beach with an armful of fishing gear.

"Why do you want to go fishing, Lucy?" asked Grandpa as he dragged the fishing boat into shallow water.

"To find your teeth, of course," said Lucy.

"How are you going to do that?" asked Grandpa, climbing into the boat after Lucy.

"You'll see," smiled Lucy. "It's a surprise."

The boat bobbed up and down over the waves as Lucy and Grandpa headed out to sea.

"Are we there yet? Is this the spot?" asked Grandpa, staring into the water.

Lucy pulled a map out of her pocket and studied it. "Yes, this is it."

Grandpa grabbed his fishing rod. He put a shrimp on his hook. Lucy grabbed her fishing rod. Then she pulled a metal box from her pocket. She tied it to the end of her fishing line.

"Isn't that *Doggie's Little Helper?*" asked Grandpa. "How's that going to find my teeth?"

"It used to be *Doggie's Little Helper,* but I've fixed it. Now it finds false teeth instead of dog bones," said Lucy.

Grandpa's mouth fell open. "Awesome, Lucy."

"I figured out that your false teeth have drifted to somewhere near here," said Lucy.

"And that thing's going to find them! Super!" cried Grandpa.

Chapter 4

Fish with a Grin

Grandpa and Lucy dropped their lines over the side. They fished for an hour. Grandpa caught seven fish. Lucy caught seven plastic bags!

"I don't get it," said Lucy as she checked her invention. "This thing looks OK. I don't know why it's catching plastic bags. I'll try again."

They fished for another hour. Grandpa caught
eight fish. Lucy caught eight car tires!

"I don't understand," sighed Lucy, scratching
her head. "Something must be wrong with it."
Lucy fiddled with her invention. She unscrewed
bolts and twisted wires. She adjusted a tiny
dial. "There! That should do it. Now I'll find
your teeth, Grandpa."

Lucy dropped her fishing line over the side of the boat with her invention on the end of it.

Grandpa's shoulders drooped. "I don't know, Lucy. I think it's hopeless. We'll never find them," he muttered. "I've lost my lovely, white, sparkling smile forever."

Just then Lucy felt something tugging on her line. "I've got something!" she yelled.

Grandpa looked. A huge fish was splashing and thrashing on the end of Lucy's line.
"It's a fish, Lucy! A beauty!"

"I should be catching teeth, not fish!" said Lucy, frowning as she reeled it in. The fish landed with a thud in the bottom of the boat.

"What a whopper!" yelled Grandpa as he put his foot on it.

"I hope you didn't break my invention," Lucy said to the fish. The fish grinned back at Lucy.

"Grandpa! Look!" cried Lucy.

Grandpa's eyes nearly popped out of his head. "The fish is wearing my teeth!" he shouted.

Grandpa hugged Lucy. "You're the best inventor ever!" He grabbed his false teeth from the fish and put them in his mouth. "That's much better." Grandpa gave a dazzling smile. "Lucy, I've got the coolest name for your invention."

"What is it?" asked Lucy.

Grandpa chuckled. "Barney's bone-finding invention was called *Doggie's Little Helper*. This invention finds teeth, so we should call it *Grandpa's Little Helper!*"

Glossary

adjusted
changed slightly

automatic
able to move by itself

crest
the top part of a wave

drifted
carried along by water

inventor
a person who thinks of
and makes something
new

jiffy
a very short time

legend
a person who is famous
for doing something well

swell
a long, unbroken wave

test run
the first try

tube
the hollow part of a
breaking wave

Jenny Dobbie

I wish that I owned some of Lucy's inventions like *Crazy Cleaner* and *The Easy Surfer*. If I did, I would set *Crazy Cleaner* to "clean house," grab *The Easy Surfer,* and race down to the beach.

It would be great fun zipping in and out of the surf and riding the tube. I might even try a handstand! Everyone would want a turn on *The Easy Surfer* — including Grandpa!

But perhaps he'd better leave his teeth at home!

Craig Smith